Emily
Dickinson

AMERICAN WOMEN of ACHIEVEMENT

Emily Dickinson

VICTORIA OLSEN

CHELSE ... ISHERS

Chelsea House Publishers
EDITOR-IN-CHIEF Nancy Toff
EXECUTIVE EDITOR Remmel T. Nunn
MANAGING EDITOR Karyn Gullen Browne
COPY CHIEF Juliann Barbato
PICTURE EDITOR Adrian G. Allen
ART DIRECTOR Maria Epes
MANUFACTURING MANAGER Gerald Levine

American Women of Achievement
SENIOR EDITOR Richard Rennert

Staff for EMILY DICKINSON
TEXT EDITOR Will Broaddus
COPY EDITOR Philip Koslow
DEPUTY COPY CHIEF Mark Rifkin
EDITORIAL ASSISTANT Nicole Claro
PICTURE RESEARCHER Sue Biederman
ASSISTANT ART DIRECTOR Loraine Machlin
DESIGNER Debora Smith
PRODUCTION MANAGER Joseph Romano
PRODUCTION COORDINATOR Marie Claire Cebrián
COVER ART Lisa Desimini

9 8

Library of Congress Cataloging-in-Publication Data

Olsen, Victoria.
    Emily Dickinson, poet/by Victoria Olsen.
        p.   cm.—(American women of achievement)
    Includes bibliographical references.
    Summary: Follows the life of the reclusive nineteenth-
century poet from Amherst, Massachusetts.
    ISBN 1-55546-649-4
        0-7910-0431-7 (pbk.)
    1. Dickinson, Emily, 1830–1886—Biography—Juvenile
literature. 2. Poets, American—19th century—Biography—
Juvenile literature. [1. Dickinson, Emily, 1830–
1886. 2. Poets, American.] I. Title. II. Series.
PS1541.Z5047 1990
811'.4—dc20   89-71168
[B]   CIP
[92]   AC

CONTENTS

WOMEN of ACHIEVEMENT

Jane Addams
SOCIAL WORKER

Madeleine Albright
STATESWOMAN

Marian Anderson
SINGER

Susan B. Anthony
WOMAN SUFFRAGIST

Clara Barton
AMERICAN RED CROSS FOUNDER

Margaret Bourke-White
PHOTOGRAPHER

Rachel Carson
BIOLOGIST AND AUTHOR

Cher
SINGER AND ACTRESS

Hillary Rodham Clinton
FIRST LADY AND ATTORNEY

Katie Couric
JOURNALIST

Diana, Princess of Wales
HUMANITARIAN

Emily Dickinson
POET

Elizabeth Dole
POLITICIAN

Amelia Earhart
AVIATOR

Gloria Estefan
SINGER

Jodie Foster
ACTRESS AND DIRECTOR

Betty Friedan
FEMINIST

Althea Gibson
TENNIS CHAMPION

Ruth Bader Ginsburg
SUPREME COURT JUSTICE

Helen Hayes
ACTRESS

Katharine Hepburn
ACTRESS

Mahalia Jackson
GOSPEL SINGER

Helen Keller
HUMANITARIAN

**Ann Landers/
Abigail Van Buren**
COLUMNISTS

Barbara McClintock
BIOLOGIST

Margaret Mead
ANTHROPOLOGIST

Edna St. Vincent Millay
POET

Julia Morgan
ARCHITECT

Toni Morrison
AUTHOR

Grandma Moses
PAINTER

Lucretia Mott
WOMAN SUFFRAGIST

Sandra Day O'Connor
SUPREME COURT JUSTICE

Rosie O'Donnell
ENTERTAINER AND COMEDIAN

Georgia O'Keeffe
PAINTER

Eleanor Roosevelt
DIPLOMAT AND HUMANITARIAN

Wilma Rudolph
CHAMPION ATHLETE

Elizabeth Cady Stanton
WOMAN SUFFRAGIST

Harriet Beecher Stowe
AUTHOR AND ABOLITIONIST

Barbra Streisand
ENTERTAINER

Elizabeth Taylor
ACTRESS AND ACTIVIST

Mother Teresa
HUMANITARIAN AND
RELIGIOUS LEADER

Barbara Walters
JOURNALIST

Edith Wharton
AUTHOR

Phyllis Wheatley
POET

Oprah Winfrey
ENTERTAINER

Babe Didrikson Zaharias
CHAMPION ATHLETE

"Remember the Ladies"

MATINA S. HORNER

Remember the Ladies." That is what Abigail Adams wrote to her husband John, then a delegate to the Continental Congress, as the Founding Fathers met in Philadelphia to form a new nation in March of 1776. "Be more generous and favorable to them than your ancestors. Do not put such unlimited power in the hands of the Husbands. If particular care and attention is not paid to the Ladies," Abigail Adams warned, "we are determined to foment a Rebellion, and will not hold ourselves bound by any Laws in which we have no voice, or Representation."

The words of Abigail Adams, one of the earliest American advocates of women's rights, were prophetic. Because when we have not "remembered the ladies," they have, by their words and deeds, reminded us so forcefully of the omission that we cannot fail to remember them. For the history of American women is as interesting and varied as the history of our nation as a whole. American women have played an integral part in founding, settling, and building our country. Some we remember as remarkable women who—against great odds—achieved distinction in the public arena: Anne Hutchinson, who in the 17th century became a charismatic religious leader; Phillis Wheatley, an 18th-century black slave who became a poet; Susan B. Anthony, whose name is synonymous with the 19th-century women's rights movement, and who led the struggle to enfranchise women; and, in our own century, Amelia Earhart, the first woman to cross the Atlantic Ocean by air.

These extraordinary women certainly merit our admiration, but other women, "common women," many of them all but forgotten, should also be recognized for their contributions to American thought and culture. Women have been community builders; they have founded schools and formed voluntary associations to help those in need; they have assumed the major responsibility for rearing children, passing on from one generation to the next the values that keep a culture alive. These and innumerable other contributions, once ignored, are now being recognized by scholars, students, and the public. It is exciting and gratifying to realize that a part of our history that was hardly acknowledged a few generations ago is now being studied and brought to light.

In recent decades, the field of women's history has grown from obscurity to a politically controversial splinter movement to academic respectability, in many cases mainstreamed into such traditional disciplines as history, economics, and psychology. Scholars of women, both female and male, have organized research centers at such prestigious institutions as Wellesley College, Stanford University, and the University of California. Other notable centers for women's studies are the Center for the American Woman and Politics at the Eagleton Institute of Politics at Rutgers University; the Henry A. Murray Research Center for the Study of Lives, at Radcliffe College; and the Women's Research and Education Institute, the research arm of the Congressional Caucus on Women's Issues. Other scholars and public figures have established archives and libraries, such as the Schlesinger Library on the History of Women in America, at Radcliffe College, and the Sophia Smith Collection, at Smith College, to collect and preserve the written and tangible legacies of women.

From the initial donation of the Women's Rights Collection in 1943, the Schlesinger Library grew to encompass vast collections documenting the manifold accomplishments of American women. Simultaneously, the women's movement in general and the academic discipline of women's studies in particular also began with a narrow definition and gradually expanded their mandate. Early causes such as woman suffrage and social reform, abolition and organized labor were joined by newer concerns such as the history of women in business and the professions and in politics and government; the study of the family; and social issues such as health policy and education.

Women, as historian Arthur M. Schlesinger, jr., once pointed out, "have constituted the most spectacular casualty of traditional history. They have made up at least half the human race, but you could never tell that by looking at the books historians write." The new breed of historians is remedying that omission. They have written books about immigrant women and about working-class women who struggled for survival in cities and about black women who met the challenges of life in rural areas. They are telling the stories of women who, despite the barriers of tradition and economics, became lawyers and doctors and public figures.

The women's studies movement has also led scholars to question traditional interpretations of their respective disciplines. For example, the study of war has traditionally been an exercise in military and political analysis, an examination of strategies planned and executed by men. But scholars of women's history have pointed out that wars have also been periods of tremendous change and even opportunity for women, because the very absence of men on the home front enabled them to expand their educational, economic, and professional activities and to assume leadership in their homes.

The early scholars of women's history showed a unique brand of courage in choosing to investigate new subjects and take new approaches to old ones. Often, like their subjects, they endured criticism and even ostracism by their academic colleagues. But their efforts have unquestionably been worthwhile, because with the publication of each new study and book another piece of the historical patchwork is sewn into place, revealing an increasingly comprehensive picture of the role of women in our rich and varied history.

Such books on groups of women are essential, but books that focus on the lives of individuals are equally indispensable. Biographies can be inspirational, offering their readers the example of people with vision who have looked outside themselves for their goals and have often struggled against great obstacles to achieve them. Marian Anderson, for instance, had to overcome racial bigotry in order to perfect her art and perform as a concert singer. Isadora Duncan defied the rules of classical dance to find true artistic freedom. Jane Addams had to break down society's notions of the proper role for women in order to create new social institutions, notably the settlement house. All of these women had to come to terms both with themselves and with the world in which they lived. Only then could they move ahead as pioneers in their chosen callings.

Biography can inspire not only by adulation but also by realism. It helps us to see not only the qualities in others that we hope to emulate, but also, perhaps, the weaknesses that made them "human." By helping us identify with the subject on a more personal level they help us to feel that we, too, can achieve such goals. We read about Eleanor Roosevelt, for instance, who occupied a unique and seemingly enviable position as the wife of the president. Yet we can sympathize with her inner dilemma: an inherently shy woman, she had to force herself to live a most public life in order to use her position to benefit others. We may not be able to imagine ourselves having the immense poetic talent of Emily Dickinson, but from her story we can understand the challenges faced by a creative woman who was expected to fulfill many family responsibilities. And though few of us will ever reach the level of athletic accomplishment displayed by Wilma Rudolph or Babe Zaharias, we can still appreciate their spirit, their overwhelming will to excel.

A biography is a multifaceted lens. It is first of all a magnification, the intimate examination of one particular life. But at the same time, it is a wide-angle lens, informing us about the world in which the subject lived. We come away from reading about one life knowing more about the social, political, and economic fabric of the time. It is for this reason, perhaps, that the great New England essayist Ralph Waldo Emerson wrote, in 1841, "There is properly no history: only biography." And it is also why biography, and particularly women's biography, will continue to fascinate writers and readers alike.

Emily Dickinson

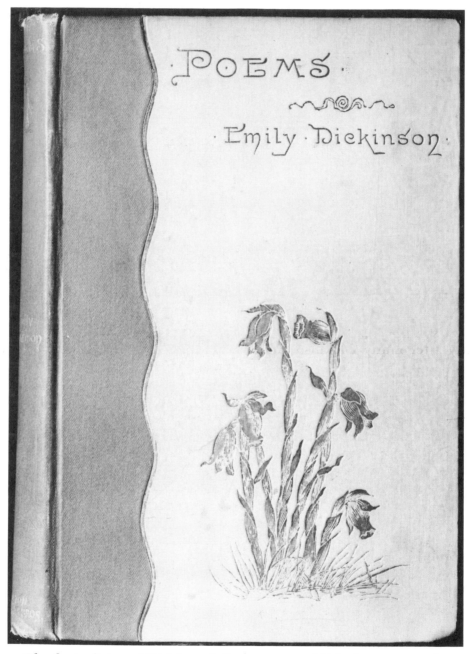

The first edition of Dickinson's Poems *was published in 1890 and contained 116 selections. It was not until more than a half century later that all 1,775 of her poems were published.*

ONE

Hide-and-Seek

Shortly after Emily Dickinson died at the age of 55 in 1886, her sister, Lavinia, made a momentous discovery. While sorting through Emily's belongings in their large house in Amherst, Massachusetts, Lavinia stumbled on hundreds of poems in a locked chest in her sister's room. Eager to have her sister's poetry published, Lavinia brought the manuscripts to her sister-in-law, Susan Gilbert Dickinson, who had been something of a mentor to Emily. But when Susan expressed little enthusiasm for undertaking the project—she felt that the public would not care for the poems—Lavinia decided to show them to her neighbor and friend Mabel Loomis Todd, who was also acquainted with Emily's writing.

In recalling the night that Lavinia Dickinson brought the poems to her, Todd said that Lavinia was "trembling with excitement" at her discovery. She had been given strict orders by Emily Dickinson to burn all her letters and other manuscripts after her death, and Lavinia had loyally obeyed these directions. But, according to Todd, Lavinia "had had no instructions to destroy" these newly found poems. Instead, she thrust the disorganized pile of manuscripts at Todd, who was also a writer, and persuaded her to arrange for their publication.

During her lifetime, Emily Dickinson had published only seven poems, all anonymously. "If fame belonged to me," she explained to a friend in 1862, "I could not escape her.... My Barefoot-Rank is better." Nevertheless, Lavinia was determined to see her sister's poems appear in print.

Throughout Dickinson's life, her sister, Lavinia (shown here), was the poet's staunchest ally. Like Emily, Lavinia never married and spent almost her entire life in the family home in Amherst, Massachusetts.

It was not an easy task, however. To begin with, the poet's nearly illegible handwriting had to be deciphered. Emily Dickinson had also sprinkled her poems with dashes, asterisks, crosses, and alternate word choices that made them even harder to read. And then there was the problem of organiz-

ing such a large collection in which very few of the poems were titled or dated.

Emily Dickinson had bundled her early poems into booklets of paper that she had sewn together. When Lavinia found the cache of verses, there were about 40 of these booklets, each containing about 20 poems. As Emily had grown older, however, she had stopped making booklets and had jotted down her poems on single sheets of paper, scraps of newspaper, fragments of envelopes, and anything else that was within reach when inspiration struck. Mabel Loomis Todd worked full-time to recopy and organize the piles of paper while she searched for a publisher for Emily Dickinson's poems.

The first person Todd sought out was Thomas Wentworth Higginson, a prominent figure in American letters. He had first crossed paths with Emily Dickinson almost 25 years earlier, in April 1862, the same month that the *Atlantic Monthly* had published his essay, "Letter to a Young Contributor." The article offered practical advice to aspiring authors, and among the readers it inspired was Emily Dickinson, then a young and hopeful poet.

Believing that Higginson would be a valuable person to consult about getting one's poetry published, Dickinson immediately sent him four poems with an unsigned note that asked: "Mr. Higginson, Are you too deeply occupied to say if my Verse is alive? The Mind is so near itself—it cannot see distinctly— and I have none to ask—" She included

A fragment of a poem that Dickinson wrote on an envelope flap. At first, she entered her poems neatly in notebooks; but in later years, she composed her verse on assorted scraps of paper.

a small envelope with the note and poems. Inside the envelope was a card that bore her name.

Higginson was not sure what to make of this unusual package. He was especially puzzled by the poems; written in an unconventional, aphoristic style, they left him mystified. Indeed, they bore little resemblance to the sentimental verse that was popular at the time. Nevertheless, Higginson wrote back to Dickinson, wanting to know more about her life and asking if he could see more samples of her work.

Dickinson had already published two of her poems, "I taste a liquor never brewed" and "Safe in their Alabaster Chambers," in a prominent Massachusetts newspaper, the *Springfield Republican*. But she had become incensed by the editorial changes her poetry had undergone in an attempt to make her verse "more fashionable." It was her hope that Higginson could get her poetry into print without having it altered in a manner that she found totally unacceptable.

Dickinson had every reason to believe she had found a kindred spirit in Higginson. In his "Letter," Higginson advised young writers to "charge your style with life." Moreover, he was known to be a supporter of women's rights and the abolition of slavery. He seemed to flout convention, much like she did.

In response to Higginson's letter, Dickinson sent him three more of her poems and asked for additional liter-

Mabel Loomis Todd, one of Dickinson's neighbors, proved to be an instrumental figure in arranging for the publication of the poet's first book. After receiving Dickinson's manuscript of poems, Todd deciphered the cryptic handwriting, selected what poems should be printed, and then found someone to publish them.

ary advice: "Could you tell me how to grow—or is it unconveyed—like Melody—or Witchcraft?" Although Higginson never gave her the type of guidance she was looking for, he wrote her warm, supportive letters that won her confidence. Throughout their correspondence in the years that followed, he proved to be, as Dickinson later put it, her "safest friend."

Higginson had never seen most of the poems Todd sent him, however, and he surveyed them with amazement. According to Todd, he said that "he had no idea there were so many in passably conventional form, and if I would classify them . . . he would look them over later in the winter." Several months thereafter, in early 1890, he selected 116 poems—those that were most like other verses of the day—and agreed to help Todd find a publisher for them.

Together, Higginson and Todd approached several publishing houses. But just about all of them seemed to think that Dickinson's unconventional poems would not sell very well. One prominent publisher even went so far as to say that the poems were "queer—the rhymes were all wrong."

Yet Todd eventually found someone who was willing to take a chance. Thomas Niles of Roberts Brothers, a Boston-based firm that had previously published one of Dickinson's poems in an anthology, agreed to print a selection of her verse, although under one condition: Lavinia Dickinson had to cover the printing costs. Eager to see

"I could only sit still and watch, as one does in the woods," author and critic Thomas Wentworth Higginson said of Dickinson after serving for 25 years as her close friend and mentor.

the poems published, Lavinia readily agreed to the deal.

The first volume of Emily Dickinson's *Poems* was published that same year, in 1890. Four hundred eighty copies were printed. To almost everyone's surprise, the edition sold out immediately.

Over the next six months, there was a demand for six more printings. Five more printings sold out by 1892. And by 1894, almost 20,000 copies had been sold.

After this successful debut, Todd and Higginson, who had coedited the first volume of Dickinson's verse, worked feverishly to make her remaining poems available to a growing audience. As each new selection of poems was published, the public and critics alike praised the freshness of Dickinson's simple rhythms, unusual rhymes, and vivid imagery. After a lifetime of obscurity, Emily Dickinson had finally emerged as a powerful new voice in American poetry.

Executed by Charles Temple, a native
of Smyrna.
1845

Emily E. Dickinson

This silhouette is one of the few known likenesses of Dickinson.

T W O

"She Is a Very Good Child"

Emily Elizabeth Dickinson was born on December 10, 1830, in a large brick house built by her paternal grandfather on Main Street in Amherst, Massachusetts. She was the second child of Emily Norcross and Edward Dickinson, who had had a son, William Austin, two years earlier. A third child, Lavinia Norcross, was born when Emily was two years old.

Members of the Dickinson clan first came to America from England in 1630, and Emily and her siblings were members of the third generation of Dickinsons born in Amherst. Nestled in the rich farmland of the Connecticut River valley in western Massachusetts, the small town of Amherst was a peaceful community. Farmers, owners of small businesses, and professionals made up most of the population. Yet at the time of Emily's birth, this quiet town was surrounded by a rapidly changing society. New inventions enabled farmers to grow more crops while employing fewer laborers, and young people flocked from the countryside to booming cities, where advances in mechanization aided the development of factories. Cities became manufacturing centers filled with workers from rural areas and immigrants from Europe.

The United States also increased in size during this period, acquiring the huge territories that now make up the Midwest. In the 1800s, this land was cheap and plentiful, and it lured a number of pioneers, including a few Amherst residents who journeyed west to try their hand at farming the fertile plains. The Dickinsons remained firmly ensconced in Amherst, however, and cherished their achievements and traditions.

The town of Amherst in the early 1840s. The Amherst Academy, a school that Dickinson attended for eight years, is the second building from the right.

By 20th-century standards, the living conditions in Amherst during Emily Dickinson's childhood seem primitive. When she was a girl, Amherst consisted of 40 houses and 4 dirt roads. Many families raised chickens in their backyard, kept cows, and grew their own vegetables. The Dickinsons owned carriage horses, as did most of the town's more affluent families. Townspeople chopped their own wood to fuel stoves and fireplaces for cooking and heating, and they pumped their water from nearby wells.

Because there was no system for purifying water or treating sewage, out-breaks of typhoid and cholera—two serious illnesses spread through contaminated water—were fairly frequent. Nineteenth-century medicine had neither cures for nor vaccines against these maladies, and doctors were helpless when faced with such contagious diseases as malaria, pneumonia, smallpox, and tuberculosis, which were all common. Even simple injuries and illnesses could quickly become life threatening, and the death rate, especially among children, was high.

A typical New England Puritan community, Amherst was unique in several ways. Tucked into the Connecticut

River valley and ringed by mountains, the town was situated in extremely beautiful countryside. Residents could enjoy stunning views of the thickly forested, rolling hills that surrounded them. But Amherst's most extraordinary feature was the college that Emily's grandfather Samuel Fowler Dickinson had helped to found.

Established in 1821 to train orthodox Congregational ministers, Amherst College was responsible for bringing a number of remarkable scholars to the area. All the townspeople felt the influence of the college, especially the Dickinsons, who were closely associated with it. Emily's father as well as her brother attended the college, and each later served as its treasurer.

The treasury of the college was often empty, however. Trying to keep the newly founded institution afloat was

Dickinson was born, spent most of her life, and died in this house in Amherst. Known as the Homestead, it was built by her paternal grandfather.

an expensive proposition, and Samuel Fowler Dickinson, a successful lawyer, eventually exhausted his income and savings. When his money ran out, he donated his horses to help with the construction of the school and allowed the laborers who needed a place to live to stay in his house. His zeal for education caused his health and his business to suffer so much that by 1830 he was on the verge of bankruptcy.

In an effort to make ends meet, the three generations of Dickinsons then in Amherst shared the large Main Street house, known as the Homestead. Edward Dickinson and his growing family occupied the west side of the house while the rest of the family lived on the east side. At times, the Homestead sheltered as many as 13 family members. Consequently, Emily spent her first few years in cramped, tension-filled quarters. Much of the tension stemmed from the family's increasing financial problems.

While Edward Dickinson was growing up, he was frequently affected by his father's slide into poverty. A student at Yale University in the 1820s, Edward had to return to Amherst whenever the money to pay his school bills ran short. Finally, at his father's

The Connecticut River valley in western Massachusetts, where Dickinson's hometown of Amherst is located.

urging, Edward left Yale and spent a year studying at the newly opened Amherst College.

Edward tried to help out whenever he could. After finishing college, he opened up a law practice, and by 1830 he was supporting the entire Dickinson clan. Samuel Fowler Dickinson left the family a few years later. After resorting to desperate and unsuccessful schemes to keep Amherst College in good financial order, he fled to the West, never to see his son or grandchildren again. He died in 1838 without knowing that the college had survived its precarious start.

Life did not get any easier for the Dickinsons when grandfather Samuel left Amherst. Emily's mother suffered through a difficult third pregnancy, and in February 1833 she nearly died during the delivery of her second daughter, Lavinia. Meanwhile, Edward was working long hours to make ends meet, with his law practice often keeping him far from home. When he was not away, Edward ruled the household with an iron hand. His "heart was pure and terrible," Emily later said of her father, "and I think no other like it exists."

Because of the turmoil within the Dickinson household, Emily, at the age

Emily's paternal grandfather, Samuel Fowler Dickinson, and grandmother, Lucretia Gunn Dickinson, in silhouettes made in 1828.

of two, was sent away for a few months to live with her mother's younger sister, Lavinia Norcross, who lived in Monson, Massachusetts. Lavinia Norcross delighted in caring for Emily and wrote back to Amherst that "Emily is perfectly well and contented—She is a very good child & but very little trouble—She has learned to play on the piano. . . . She has a fine appetite & sleeps well." The Norcross home was also in a bit of upheaval: In addition to tending to young Emily, Lavinia was nursing a dying relative at this time. Nevertheless, Emily was well cared for and remained in Monson until June 1833, when she returned to Amherst.

Little is known about Emily's mother, except that she was a hospitable woman whose reputation in Amherst rested on her excellent cooking and housekeeping. She was literate and well educated, even though her daughter Emily once wrote scornfully that "Mother does not care for thought." The former Emily Norcross devoted her life to family, church, and charities.

At one point, Emily Dickinson told Thomas Wentworth Higginson that she "never had a mother." But, as several biographers have pointed out, her mother was a constant presence in the house. Even though she was often ill in her later years, she continually fulfilled the numerous domestic responsibilities of a 19th-century wife and mother.

Emily Dickinson also once remarked that "I am not very well acquainted

A portrait of the poet's mother, Emily Norcross Dickinson, painted in 1840.

Dickinson's paternal grandfather cofounded Amherst College in 1821. The school originally sought to train missionaries and uphold Puritan virtues.

with father." Yet he clearly took an interest in his children's education. He was particularly proud of the academic accomplishments of his son, Austin. But Edward Dickinson also believed that women should be educated—an attitude that was not widespread in the 19th century—and both Emily and Lavinia received excellent schooling. (Emily's father was not totally liberal minded, however. Although he believed that men and women were equal in ability, he stressed that society profited most when women confined themselves to managing domestic affairs. He once wrote a series of articles for an Amherst newspaper, outlining the different spheres he believed men and women should occupy.)

Emily Dickinson began attending primary school in 1835, at the local one-room schoolhouse. Due in part to her grandfather's efforts, the Amherst school offered its students a thorough education grounded in Christian values. Emily learned to read and write using the *New England Primer*, a compilation of Christian nursery rhymes and bedtime prayers that tried to teach children to be industrious in life and spiritually prepared for death. A typical lesson in the *Primer* began, "I must obey my Lord's commands / Do something with my little hands."

Like most Amherst families, the Dickinsons were Congregationalists, members of a Protestant sect that closely followed the tenets of New En-

A view of Yale University in New Haven, Connecticut, around the time that Dickinson's father attended the college. Extremely well educated, he encouraged all three of his children to excel scholastically.

gland Puritanism. The Puritans first came to Massachusetts from England in the 1600s, seeking a haven from religious persecution. They wished to return to the original "purity" of Christianity as ordained by Jesus Christ, and they believed that this purity could be achieved by strict adherence to the values of simplicity, order, and austerity. They also showed their devotion to God through spiritual reflection, hard work, and the pursuit of education.

Each generation of the Dickinson family took its religion seriously. In his youth, Samuel Fowler Dickinson had studied to become a minister and considered his commitment to improving education part of his religious duty. Edward Dickinson, like his father, Samuel, led a life of hard work and unwavering faith that embodied Puritan values. On the mornings he was home, he always read the Bible to his family. He also presented each of his children with their own copy of the Bible. Emily received hers, with her name elaborately engraved on the cover in gilt letters, in 1843.

A religious man, Edward Dickinson could also be extremely single-minded. His father's failures had instilled in him a belief that his family must not be financially troubled ever again, and he took on a number of duties to make

In 1835, Dickinson began her formal education in this one-room schoolhouse.

Emily's father, Edward Dickinson, in addition to being a successful lawyer and politician, was a domineering parent. "If father is asleep in the lounge," Emily wrote, "the house is full."

sure that it never happened. In addition to running a flourishing law practice, he accepted several political posts and, when Emily began attending school, became Amherst College's treasurer.

All of these commitments eventually took their toll on the family. When Emily was seven years old, her father spent part of the year in Boston as a member of the Massachusetts General Court. His wife wrote him a letter in which she stated that Emily "is tired of living without a father." Nevertheless, these separations remained a part of the family's way of life. In time, Edward would continue to commit him-

Silhouettes of the Dickinson family; (from left to right) Emily Norcross, Lavinia, Austin, Emily, and Edward.

self to other projects and public offices, including two terms in the nation's capital as a U.S. congressman.

Emily Dickinson's niece, Martha Dickinson Bianchi, later described her grandfather Edward as a benevolent but remote man. When he was in Amherst, he would walk home for lunch each day. Meanwhile, his wife and two daughters would be preparing for his arrival. "No matter what the calamity," Bianchi observed, "no matter how stark the domestic emergency, by the time he reached the side piazza the peace of Heaven's own morn lay thick upon the atmosphere."

In his own home, Edward Dickinson did not have much time for his daughters. In an early letter to Thomas Wentworth Higginson, Emily complained that her father was "too busy with his Briefs—to notice what we do." Yet he was certainly capable of kind and generous acts. In fact, he gave Emily some of her most prized possessions, including a piano and a dog, Carlo. But his children were apparently uncomfortable with him. Emily once wrote that she could not tell time until she was 15 years old because her father had explained the concept to her once, but she did not understand him and was too afraid to ask him again.

When Emily Dickinson grew older, she sometimes expressed her anger at her father in subtle ways. One evening at the dinner table, her father complained that his plate had a chip in it.

Emily immediately took the plate into the backyard and smashed it into tiny pieces. Then she returned to the room, telling her father that he would never have to look at the offensive plate again.

Life in the Dickinson home was rarely so stormy. Both parents were not prone to emotional outbursts. It seems, in fact, that neither parent displayed much emotion at all. As Emily Dickinson later wrote in one of her poems:

> They shut me up in Prose
> As when a little Girl
> They put me in the Closet—
> Because they liked me "still"—
> Still!

Dickinson with her brother, Austin, and sister, Lavinia, in 1840. They remained extremely close throughout their lives.

THREE

" 'Faith' Is a Fine Invention"

By the spring of 1840, Edward Dickinson's financial situation had improved to the point where he could afford to move his wife and three children from the Homestead on Main Street to a larger house on North Pleasant Street. A few months later, Emily and her younger sister, Lavinia, started elementary school at Amherst Academy, a top private coeducational institution. Samuel Fowler Dickinson had helped to establish the school in 1814 before he shifted his attention to founding Amherst College.

The academy differed sharply from most other local schools. Nineteenth-century educators often seemed to sacrifice individual learning so that they could maintain order in the classroom. Usually, they demanded that their students learn through memorization. For-

tunately for Emily Dickinson, Amherst Academy employed the most enlightened educational principles of its day. Teachers—usually bright young graduates of nearby colleges—received careful training and were urged to use visual aids, special projects, and class trips to excite their students' interest in learning. In addition, the school encouraged informal relationships between students and teachers.

Only in theological studies was the academy more conservative than other schools of its time. The institution aimed to instill traditional Congregationalist values in its students. On this front, Emily eventually rebelled.

When nine-year-old Emily entered the academy, Amherst College had already opened its doors to academy students and encouraged them to attend classes at the college. Teachers and staff members also moved freely between the two establishments. At the academy, students handled a heavy course load that included history, geography, grammar, arithmetic, natural history, physiology, composition, chemistry, natural theology, ecclesiastical history, anatomy, astronomy, geology, and logic. Emily studied Latin, Greek, and ancient history, in addition to most of the general subjects. She also took singing and piano lessons throughout her adolescence.

In spite of her crowded schedule, Emily managed to lead an active social life. Most of her friends were smart, accomplished, and privileged. Mary and Jane Humphrey were the daughters of an Amherst College president, as was Kate Hitchcock. Emily Fowler—the granddaughter of a celebrated Amherst resident, Noah Webster, who compiled the first American dictionary—later became a published poet and biographer of her grandfather. In addition to other lively young women who were fond of reading clubs, outdoor

In the spring of 1840, the Dickinsons moved to this large house on North Pleasant Street in Amherst. Fifteen years later, however, they returned to the Homestead.

At the age of nine, Dickinson enrolled in nearby Amherst Academy, a preparatory school with an enlightened curriculum.

jaunts, and parties, Dickinson also made friends with the ambitious scholars who visited Amherst, the apprentices in her father's law office, the tutors at Amherst Academy, and the young men her brother brought home from his boarding school.

In 1844, one of Dickinson's friends, 15-year-old Sophia Holland, died from an illness. Before the burial, Emily viewed the body on its deathbed, as was customary at the time. "I shed no tear," Dickinson wrote, "for my heart was too full to weep, but after she was laid in her coffin & I felt I could not call her back again I gave way to a fixed melancholy." The depression was so severe that it preyed on Dickinson's physical health. Keeping the source of

her illness to herself, she spent a month in Boston, where she visited her aunt Lavinia and managed to regain her strength.

Although no poems from Dickinson's adolescence have survived, her letters from this period are often filled with gossip and flights of fancy. When she was 15, she noted gleefully: "I am growing handsome very fast indeed! I expect to be the belle of Amherst when I reach my 17th year. I don't doubt that I shall have perfect crowds of admirers at that age."

Dickinson may have had great expectations of herself, but no one in her family anticipated her becoming a poet. The family was not very literary minded. Edward Dickinson discour-

Among the writers whose work Dickinson admired during her youth was the English poet Elizabeth Barrett Browning.

aged his children from reading fiction; the Congregational church condemned most 19th-century fiction as frivolous. The church tolerated some New England authors, such as Nathaniel Hawthorne, and some British authors, including Charles Dickens and Sir Walter Scott. But fiction was generally considered to be a bad influence on young people.

Edward Dickinson closely monitored his family's reading habits. He did not want them to read books that "joggle the Mind." Consequently, Austin and Emily had to smuggle forbidden books into the house for what they called secret "reading feasts." Austin gave Emily a copy of Henry Wadsworth Longfellow's popular romantic novel *Kavanagh*. She also managed to get hold of books by the great English women writers of the time, including the Brontë sisters, George Eliot, and Elizabeth Barrett Browning. One author whom she refused to read, however, was the American poet Walt Whitman. She later wrote to Higginson that she had heard Whitman was "disgraceful."

Among the best-known authors of the 1840s was Ralph Waldo Emerson, who wrote such widely admired essays as "Self-Reliance" and "The Over-Soul." Until his death in 1882, he worked hard to cultivate American advances in the arts and sciences. The United States was still a very young nation when Emerson began his work, and most Americans looked to Great Britain for the latest styles and the newest ideas. Emerson became one of the first nationally known American thinkers, and by the mid-19th century he had become a spokesman for the nation as a whole.

A Massachusetts native, Emerson popularized the philosophy of transcendentalism, in which mystical individu-

The American poet Walt Whitman, who is one of the founders of modern American poetry along with Dickinson.

37

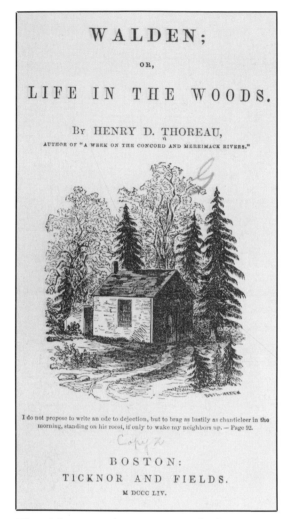

WALDEN;

OR,

LIFE IN THE WOODS.

By HENRY D. THOREAU,

AUTHOR OF "A WEEK ON THE CONCORD AND MERRIMACK RIVERS."

I do not propose to write an ode to dejection, but to brag as lustily as chanticleer in the
morning, standing on his roost, if only to wake my neighbors up. — Page 92.

BOSTON:

TICKNOR AND FIELDS.

M DCCC LIV.

The title page of Henry David Thoreau's Walden, or Life in the Woods, *a book that combined the observations of a naturalist with numerous aspects of transcendental philosophy, a very popular discipline while Dickinson was growing up.*

followers in the pratice of transcendentalism was Henry David Thoreau, who spent more than a year alone in a cabin that he built on Walden Pond in Concord, Massachusetts, in the mid-1840s. Throughout his stay at Walden, Thoreau kept a journal of his experiences and his reflections on life and nature. In 1854, he published these writings in *Walden, or Life in the Woods*, a highly acclaimed but commercially unsuccessful volume. The Dickinsons, because of their proximity to Thoreau's home and their respect for his mentor (Emerson, in fact, met the Dickinsons during one of his frequent visits to Amherst as a lecturer), were one of the few families to own a copy of *Walden*.

Despite the popularity of transcendentalism, intellectual life in Amherst was shaped chiefly by the unlikely combination of conservative Puritan ideology and a growing trend toward scientific inquiry. Nobody embodied those two contrasting strains better than Edward Hitchcock, a geologist who served as the president of Amherst College from 1845 to 1854. He taught classes at both the academy and the college for many years and influenced a generation of Amherst students with his theory of "natural religion."

A trained scientist and devout Christian, Hitchcock believed that nature revealed both God's existence and his goodwill toward humankind. The universal laws of nature worked together in perfect harmony, Hitchcock argued, and were the design of a rational God who expressed his benevolent presence

alism and visionary idealism are emphasized over the material world and empirical knowledge. One of his

A page from Dickinson's herbarium, a bound book filled with dried flowers, that she kept during her adolescence.

Edward Hitchcock, president of Amherst College from 1845 to 1854, was also a teacher and a geologist who helped instill in Dickinson a deep love of nature.

through the beauty of nature. One could see a reminder of God's goodness in every scientific observation, Hitchcock said. With great enthusiasm, he strengthened the science departments at the academy and the college and urged students to question, observe, and experiment, with the expectation that it would increase their religious understanding.

In his inaugural address as president of Amherst College in 1845, Hitchcock described the beauties of the Connecticut River valley around Amherst: "Surely if there is any poetry in the student's soul,—if any love of nature,—

they must be here developed." Although Hitchcock condemned fiction, he admired poetry, and he worked hard to communicate his love of nature and science to many of his students, including Emily Dickinson.

Like Hitchcock, Dickinson loved botany, and during her adolescence she began a herbarium—a bound book filled with dried flowers. She carefully mounted a flower on each page and then labeled it with both its English and Latin names. Dickinson was also well versed in geology, astronomy, and chemistry. At the academy, she studied with some of America's leading scientists and closely followed the scientific revolutions of her day.

Years later, Dickinson's poems would often exemplify Hitchcock's joining of precise observation and natural beauty. Scientific terms and complicated scientific theories appeared frequently in her work. In 1852, for example, she published a poem in the *Springfield Republican* that drew on Isaac Newton's discovery of gravity and other events in the history of science:

> During my education,
> It was announced to me
> That *gravitation, stumbling,*
> Fell from an *apple* tree!
> The earth upon an axis
> Was once supposed to turn,
> By way of a *gymnastic*
> In honor of the sun!
> It was the brave Columbus,
> A sailing o'er the tide,
> Who notified the nations
> Of where I would reside!

But Dickinson did not share her mentor's beliefs. To Hitchcock, science served religion as earthly evidence of God's work. Dickinson felt somewhat differently. Science seemed to reveal the inadequacy of religion. " 'Faith,' " she once wrote, "is a fine invention / When Gentlemen can *see*— / But *Microscopes* are prudent / In an Emergency."

Dickinson ended her studies at the Amherst Academy in August 1847.

During her seven years there, she was schooled to hold a particular view of religion. But she was not yet ready to embrace what she had been taught. The people of Amherst may have expected her to transform her knowledge into faith and use her power of reasoning to become the best possible wife and mother, but Emily Dickinson was determined to live up to her own expectations.

While Dickinson was growing up, religious revivals, including this one in 1840, were held throughout the Connecticut River valley to stir and satisfy religious longings. Although most of Dickinson's friends participated in these assemblies, she chose to avoid them.

FOUR

"I Love the Danger!"

Although Emily Dickinson remained somewhat isolated from the social and political changes of the early 19th century, she, her friends, and her family were deeply affected by a powerful religious movement that swept New England. In the 1840s, Protestant churches sponsored numerous revival meetings in the Connecticut River valley. At these gatherings, ministers endeavored to revive and increase the religious awareness of their listeners and stressed a return to traditional values. Whole communities enthusiastically attended revival meetings held regularly in Amherst, South Hadley, and other neighboring towns.

As a member of a prominent, devout family, Emily Dickinson was expected and encouraged to participate in revivals. Yet she seems to have deliberately avoided the assemblies. In 1844 and 1846, she failed to attend the revivals in Amherst, although her letters reveal she thought a great deal about religion.

In January 1846, 15-year-old Dickinson recounted the excitement of a revival to her friend Abiah Root and explained why she did not attend:

> The meetings were thronged by people old and young. . . . It was really wonderful to see how near heaven came to sinful mortals. Many who felt there was nothing in religion determined to go once & see if there was anything in it, and they were melted at once. . . . I attended none of the meetings last winter. . . . I felt that I was so easily excited that I might again be deceived and I dared not trust myself. Many conversed with me seriously and affectionately and I was almost inclined to yield to the claims of He who is greater than I.

At the meetings, preachers graphically contrasted the terrors of hell with the daily comfort of God's presence and the eternal bliss of salvation. They urged their congregations to confess that they were sinners, accept Jesus Christ as their savior, and conduct a Christian life. During the revivals, many people experienced religious visions that marked their "conversion" to Christianity. Although they had been born Christian and may have attended Christian services all their life, they did not become members of their church until they were admitted to it by a "profession of faith."

Conversion could be a frightening experience. A sincere conversion involved losing one's independence and utterly submitting to the will of God and the strictures of the church. Dickinson apparently found it difficult, if not impossible, to set aside the skepticism that her scientific training had instilled in her and give up her independent point of view.

Conversion did offer significant rewards to the believer who valued the lifelong security of God's love, participation in a community experience, and, most important, the promise of an afterlife that soothed one's terror of death. Belief in an afterlife was particularly attractive to the recently bereaved; many people converted while mourning loved ones.

In 1846, Abiah Root converted, but Dickinson continued to resist. She told her friend, "I can say that I never enjoyed such perfect peace and happiness as the short time in which I felt I had found my savior. But I soon forgot my morning prayer or else it was irksome to me. One by one my old habits returned and I cared less for religion than ever." Whether her resistance was a failure of faith or a triumph of self-assertion, the constant, intense pressure to convert that surrounded Dickinson troubled her for years to come.

In September 1847, when Dickinson was 16 years old, she left Amherst to attend a newly opened college for women: the Mount Holyoke Female Seminary, located in nearby South Hadley. The school had been founded and was administered by a remarkable woman named Mary Lyon, who had been a student of Edward Hitchcock's. Like Hitchcock, Lyon was an energetic and personable teacher and an inspirational leader. And, also like Hitchcock, she wanted to help save her students' souls by providing them with an orthodox Christian environment in which they could learn to accept Jesus Christ as their savior.

Lyon had not had the opportunity to begin her own education until she was an adult, but her determination ensured her speedy advancement. She had soon compiled an outstanding list of achievements, and founding Mount Holyoke ranked at the top of the list. She personally oversaw every detail of the school's management in addition to teaching chemistry and conducting daily schoolwide assemblies.

Each day, Lyon provided Mount

Abiah Root, one of Dickinson's closest friends during the poet's primary school years.

In 1847, Dickinson enrolled in the Mount Holyoke Female Seminary in nearby South Hadley, Massachusetts.

Holyoke students with a strong example of industry, integrity, and self-determination. She lived her belief that "we have great powers over ourselves. We may become almost what we will." She was very well liked by her students despite—or perhaps because of—the challenging demands she placed on them. She often reminded those who resisted conversion that she, too, had once hardened her heart against God and that her experience could give them hope for their own salvation. Dickinson, who remained plagued by doubts about her religious future,

surely heard this exhortation more than once.

Dickinson had eagerly looked forward to her year at Mount Holyoke, but once settled there she often felt homesick. She lived for brief visits from her family, who usually brought her fruit and gingerbread in addition to news from home. As soon as her family left, Dickinson would sit down and write letters urging them to visit again. She shared a room with one of her Norcross cousins and made friends easily, but her homesickness lingered. She wrote, "I am now contented & quite

happy, if I can be happy when absent from my dear home and friends."

Dickinson's daily routine at Mount Holyoke was a mixture of academic classes and religious services. She awoke at six o'clock every morning and began her day with two hours of silent devotion and private study. She attended lectures and had a calisthenics period before lunch. Each afternoon, she practiced her singing and piano playing until it was time to go to "sections," where each student reported on her own daily conduct. As Dickinson described it, "We give in all our ac-

counts for the day, including, Absence—Tardiness—Communications—Breaking Silent Study hours—Receiving Company in our rooms & ten thousand other things."

At four o'clock in the afternoon, everyone assembled to hear Mary Lyon lecture on religion. After supper, Dickinson spent another few hours in silent study until the lights were turned off at 9:45 each night. In addition to following this schedule, each student was required to help with the domestic chores of the school. Dickinson was assigned to set out, wash, and dry the

Mary Lyon, head of the Mount Holyoke Female Seminary, founded the institution in 1837 to provide students with an orthodox Christian environment. Dickinson had to follow a rigorous schedule of classes and religious services while attending the seminary.

knives used at mealtimes.

Academic standards at the school were high, and Dickinson expressed relief at having passed her first set of three-day examinations. However, religious training received the primary emphasis at Mount Holyoke. The administration quickly divided the 300 students into 3 groups: those who had converted, those who had "some hope" of conversion, and those with "no hope" of conversion at all. As more and more students became Christians, Dickinson remained one of the few who spent the year "without hope."

At Mount Holyoke, the inner turbulence of Dickinson's religious feelings and the community pressure to convert ultimately reached a crisis point. She was regularly questioned about her religious beliefs and daily instructed to save her soul. Her friends converted in increasing numbers. Abiah Root was the first, followed by a number of Dickinson's Mount Holyoke classmates.

As her year at Mount Holyoke progressed, Dickinson became more and more upset. Her homesickness increased, and her letters to Abiah took on a frantic note. On May 16, 1848, she confessed to Root that "I am not happy, and I regret that last term, when that golden opportunity was mine, that I did not give up and become a Christian. It is not now too late, so my friends tell me, so my offended conscience whispers, but it is hard for me to give up the world." By 1848, her rejection of conversion seemed fixed, and she struggled to accept the enormity of her choice.

Dickinson's health had suffered somewhat during her year at Mount Holyoke, and she spent at least a month in the spring at home in Amherst recovering from a bronchial ailment. She managed to keep up with her studies and passed all of her year-end examinations, but the summer term of 1848 was Dickinson's last at Mount Holyoke. Edward Dickinson made the actual decision not to send her back to school, but Emily did not protest.

When Dickinson returned permanently to Amherst in 1848, she found that many of her old friends had left. However, she soon discovered a new social set. A young woman named Susan Gilbert, who had spent part of her

Upon returning to Amherst from Mount Holyoke Female Seminary in 1848, Dickinson befriended Susan Gilbert (above), who married the poet's brother, Austin Dickinson, eight years later.

childhood with relatives in Amherst and then moved to New York to join other members of her family, returned to Amherst at the same time as did Dickinson. The two women soon struck up a warm friendship. Austin Dickinson was a student at Amherst College at the time, and some of his classmates and acquaintances joined Dickinson's new circle. Dickinson's sister Lavinia, known as Vinnie, remained Emily's close confidante.

Dickinson enjoyed a stimulating social life in Amherst. Over the next few years, she attended college lectures on Shakespeare, heard the world-renowned Swedish singer Jenny Lind on her only American tour, and took pleasure trips to Boston and Springfield, Massachusetts. The Dickinsons held an annual party for the graduating students of Amherst College, and Emily Dickinson was a lively hostess at these events.

The whirl of social events kept Dickinson occupied but could not completely assuage the spiritual isolation she continued to feel. Amherst was the site of yet another major religious revival in 1850, and Dickinson's friends flocked to the meetings. In August, both Edward Dickinson and Susan Gilbert converted, and in November, Lavinia Dickinson joined them.

Dickinson's letters from this period reveal her loneliness, but they no longer indicate struggle. She seems to have chosen her path at Mount Holyoke, and in Amherst she was forced to confront the implications of her decision. In the midst of the revival, she lamented: "Christ is calling everyone here, all my companions have answered, even my darling Vinnie be-

In 1850, Dickinson attended a performance by singer Jenny Lind, "the Swedish Nightingale," who had been brought to America by carnival promoter P. T. Barnum.

lieves she loves, and trusts him, and I am standing alone in rebellion. . . . I can't tell *what* they have found, but *they* think it is something precious. I wonder if it *is?*"

Her doubts about religion persisted, and she often expressed her torment in verse:

> I shall know why—when Time is
>   over—
> And I have ceased to wonder why—
> Christ will explain each separate
>   anguish
> In the fair schoolroom of the sky—
> He will tell me what "Peter"
>   promised—
> And I—for wonder at his woe—
> I shall forget the drop of Anguish
> That scalds me now—that scalds me
>   now!

By the end of the year, Dickinson had made some sort of peace with her decision. She never rejected spiritual inquiry and would continue to ponder questions of faith, death, and immortality for the rest of her life, although she refused to participate in the religious rites of her community. In 1860, she ceased going to church altogether.

But by 1850, Dickinson had already demonstrated the strength of her will. At the age of 19, she had put Mary Lyon's maxim that "we may become almost what we will" to an unexpected use; for better or worse, she had taken an independent stand on the issue of faith. "The shore is safer, Abiah," she confessed in a letter to her friend, "but I love to buffet the sea. . . . I love the danger!"

Dickinson's brother, Austin, around 1854, when he returned to Amherst after graduating from Harvard Law School. During the four years that he lived in Boston, Emily wrote to him almost every day.

FIVE

"Home Is Bright and Shining"

As 19-year-old Emily Dickinson struggled with her religious doubts, she had the good fortune to be surrounded by the company of her tightly knit family. Her sister, Lavinia, was a bright, witty, and fun-loving companion. And so was their beloved brother, Austin, who lived at home until 1850, when he moved to Boston for several years. Presiding over the family was Edward Dickinson, a well-respected, prosperous lawyer whose political career was gaining momentum.

During this time, only the declining health of Emily Norcross Dickinson marred the family's happiness. She had never been robust and throughout the years suffered bouts of "nervous illness." She became increasingly debilitated and spent more and more time confined to her bed. Her daughters took over the household chores of cooking, sewing, cleaning, and gardening, in addition to caring for their mother.

The difficulties of this period brought Emily closer to Lavinia, who in later years became her elder sister's chief supporter and a fervent defender of the family. Lavinia may have shared her sister's verbal talents, but she used them socially; she was a pleasant and entertaining conversationalist who appears to have been in great demand as a guest. Her diary for 1851 lists hundreds of social engagements, many of which Emily probably attended as well.

Joseph Lyman, a former classmate of Austin Dickinson's, was one of Lavinia Dickinson's suitors before he moved away from Amherst in 1851. During the years that followed, he frequently corresponded with Emily Dickinson.

Lavinia had several suitors during these years, but the one she favored, Joseph Lyman, left New England and moved to the South.

Emily Dickinson had always been close to Austin, and after he left for Boston in 1850 she compensated for his absence by writing to him nearly every day until his return in 1854. In her letters, she constantly urged him to come back to Amherst, reminding him that "home is bright and shining." Like Emily, Austin was gifted, articulate, and intensely emotional, and he suffered a crisis of faith similar to hers, although it seems that they never spoke to each other about their religious doubts.

Their relationship had a competitive side. Emily Dickinson could be fierce in her demand for attention, as a letter to her brother, dated October 1850, shows: "Permit me to tie your shoe, to run like a dog behind you. I can bark, see here! Bow wow! Now if that isn't fine I don't know! Permit me to be a stick, to show how I will not beat you, a stone, how I will not fling, mosquito, I will not sting." Once, when he sent her a poem he had written, she warned him that "I've been in the habit *myself* of writing some few things, and it rather appears to me that you're getting away with my patent, so you'd better be somewhat careful, or I'll call the police!"

Dickinson wrote poetry throughout the 1850s. Writing valentines was a popular literary exercise in those days, and several of Emily's were published to high acclaim. One recipient of Dickinson's valentines was George Gould, the editor of the Amherst College *Indicator*. Some biographers suggest he was an early suitor of Dickinson's, although the two may have carried on a purely literary friendship. Whatever their relationship, she sent him the following valentine, in which she mixed prose and poetry:

Magnum bonum, "harum scarum," zounds et zounds, et war alarum, man reformam, life perfectum, mundum changum, all things flarum?

Sir, I desire an interview; meet me at sunrise, or sunset, or the new moon—the place is immaterial. In gold, or in purple, or sackcloth—I look not upon the *raiment*. With sword, or with pen, or with plough—the weapons are less than the *wielder*. In coach, or in wagon, or walking, the *equipage* far from the *man*. With soul, or spirit, or body, they are all alike to me. With host or alone, in sunshine or storm, in heaven or earth, *some* how or *no* how—I propose, sir, to see you.

The rest of the valentine includes extravagant allusions to biblical myth, American politics, and whatever else popped into Dickinson's head. Gould published the piece anonymously in the February 1850 issue of the *Indicator*, and it was very well received. Another of her valentines was published two years later in the *Springfield Republican*.

Composing valentines was a valuable literary exercise for Dickinson. In addition, she corresponded with several people who may have influenced her development as a writer. She had already made important decisions about her life—the most crucial of which was probably her refusal to convert—but her life as a poet continued to evolve during the early 1850s. Several of her friends may have been interested in her poetry and helped her to refine it. Ben-

jamin Newton, an apprentice in her father's law office from 1847 to 1849, exchanged letters with Dickinson until his early death in 1853. He praised her literary talent when he commented in her autograph book that "all can write Autographs, but few paragraphs."

Leonard Humphrey, who had been a tutor and principal of the Amherst Academy during Dickinson's years there, also took an interest in poetry and may have encouraged Dickinson to

George Gould, editor of the Amherst College Indicator, *was the first person to print one of Dickinson's poems. He published a valentine by her in the February 1850 issue.*

Austin and Susan Gilbert Dickinson's small estate in Amherst, the Evergreens. The illustration on the opposite page shows the proximity of the Homestead (center, above the word Main*) to the Evergreens (to the left of the Homestead).*

write. (However, he too died at an early age, in 1850.) Dickinson exchanged poems with Henry Vaughan Emmons, a student at Amherst College from 1850 to 1854. Joseph Lyman, who was a frequent guest at the Dickinsons' home as Austin and Emily's friend and Lavinia's suitor, also had literary ambitions. After he left Amherst in 1851, he and Dickinson began a lifelong correspondence, and he remained an admirer of Dickinson's literary style.

Part of Dickinson's bond with Susan Gilbert was a mutual appreciation of literature. Like Dickinson's other friends, Susan Gilbert was well educated and intelligent, and she and Dickinson seem to have been intellectually well matched. For many years, they shared an intense and sometimes strained friendship. Such friendships between women were common in the 19th century. Because relations with men were often restricted, women were

accustomed to relying on the emotional support of other women, creating friendships that often became the most sustained and rewarding ties in a woman's life.

In 1851, just one year after Austin left for Boston, Gilbert took a teaching job in Baltimore for a year, and Dickinson's letters express how distraught she was at her friend's absence: "Oh my darling one, how long you wander from me, how weary I grow of waiting and looking, and calling for you; sometimes I shut my eyes, and shut my heart towards you, and try hard to forget you because you grieve me so, but you'll never go away, Oh you never will—say, Susie, promise me again, and I will smile faintly—and take up my little cross again of sad—*sad* separation."

Dickinson's fears about permanent separation from Susan Gilbert turned out to be groundless. Gilbert returned from Baltimore in the summer of 1852, and over the next few years she and Austin Dickinson conducted a stormy courtship, which resulted in their marriage in 1856. After the wedding, she lived next door to Emily Dickinson for the rest of the poet's life. Dickinson encouraged the match; indeed, Gilbert was popular with most of the Dickinsons.

Dickinson's relationship with Gilbert was not entirely placid, however. Gilbert never replied to letters as often as Dickinson wished her to, and Dickinson sometimes complained of neglect. Gradually, Dickinson's protective younger sister, Lavinia, broke with Susan over her treatment of Emily, and in 1854, Dickinson herself sent her friend an ultimatum: "Sue—you can go or stay—There is but one alternative— We differ often lately, and this must be the last." Their relationship resumed shortly afterward, but tensions between them surfaced again and again throughout their long association.

Religion may have played a part in this disagreement. Gilbert was already engaged to Austin Dickinson in 1854, but her anxiety about Austin's religious faith made her delay their wedding plans. Gilbert knew that Emily Dickinson sympathized with her brother's religious doubts, and this may have disrupted the friendship between the two women. Gilbert's objections disappeared when Austin converted in January 1856, and the couple married in July. Oddly, none of Austin's relatives attended the wedding, which took place in upstate New York.

The mid-1850s proved to be a time of great change for the entire Dickinson family. Edward Dickinson was doing well financially and was enjoying a string of public successes, including having a hand in the construction of the Amherst-Belchertown railroad. In 1852, he had achieved his highest ambition when he was elected to the U.S. Congress as a representative from Massachusetts, and he wound up serving two terms as a member of the conservative Whig party.

Even though Edward Dickinson's new duties took him far from home, in the spring of 1855 he decided to purchase the Homestead along with 13 acres of surrounding property. That November, the family moved back to the house where Emily had been born. While Austin Dickinson was away at Harvard Law School from 1853 to 1854 and engaged to Susan Gilbert, he seriously considered moving from Amherst to settle in the Midwest. His plan threw the close-knit family into a panic, and Edward Dickinson quickly offered to build a house for the young couple right next door to the Homestead if Austin would agree to start his law practice in Amherst. Austin accepted, and in the summer of 1856 he and Susan Gilbert Dickinson moved into the home they called the Evergreens.

By that time, Emily Dickinson had also experienced a change of scene. In the spring of 1855, she took a trip to Philadelphia and Washington, D.C., where she visited her father. It was to be the longest journey that she ever made in her life.

Dickinson enjoyed the trip despite experiencing her usual homesickness. While in Philadelphia, it is possible

In the spring of 1855, Dickinson traveled to Philadelphia and Washington, D.C. (shown here), to visit her father, who had become a U.S. congressman. The trip marked her last major journey away from Amherst.

that she met a charismatic young preacher named Charles Wadsworth, with whom some biographers believe she was romantically involved. A few years after her visit, she began a correspondence with Wadsworth that lasted until his death in 1882. There were, however, obstacles to a romance between them. For one thing, Wadsworth was a married man; for another, he moved to San Francisco in 1862. Only two meetings between Dickinson and Wadsworth have been verified, occurring when he visited Amherst in 1860 and 1880. Nonetheless, Dickinson's niece, Martha Dickinson Bianchi, believed that Wadsworth was Emily Dickinson's "fate" and argued that the two fell in love at first sight, then tragically separated.

In the spring of 1858, Dickinson did write an emotional letter to an unidentified friend. It was the first of three such letters, addressed only to her "Master," that have inspired much speculation into Dickinson's love life during this turbulent period. All three were found among her papers after her death, and it is unknown whether she mailed copies of the letters or not. Dickinson began the first one, "I am ill, but grieving more that you are ill," proceeded to respond to an earlier letter, and bemoaned her separation from the intended recipient. The few other letters from this period also reveal her unhappiness.

Dickinson's life began to change in the second half of the 1850s. Her increasing production of poetry corresponded to her declining social life, although the change occurred gradually. In 1857, she participated in the Amherst Agricultural Fair, where her rye bread won second prize, and in 1858 she sat on the planning committee for the annual Amherst Cattle Show. But by the end of the decade, her preference for seclusion had begun to emerge.

It has been suggested that while Dickinson visited Philadelphia in 1855, she met Charles Wadsworth (above), pastor of the Arch Street Presbyterian Church (opposite). In any event, Dickinson and Wadsworth established a steady correspondence a few years later.

Scribners *magazine editor Josiah Holland was another of Dickinson's literary acquaintances. His wife, Elizabeth, was Dickinson's steadiest correspondent over the years.*

A failed romance is a tempting explanation for Dickinson's brooding depression during this period. A number of events could have distressed her. Her brother had just married her best friend, and she may have felt excluded by the relationship that she had once encouraged. Many of her friends had married and moved away: Emily Fowler in 1853, Abiah Root in 1854, and Abby Wood in 1855, among others.

Dickinson did make a few important new friends in the 1850s, including Josiah and Elizabeth Holland. Josiah Holland was an author and journalist, but despite his literary interests, Dickinson was closer to his wife, Elizabeth. Dickinson even visited her in Springfield in 1853. When Josiah Holland moved to New York City to found his own magazine in 1866, Dickinson exchanged letters with Elizabeth Holland regularly. Over the years, Elizabeth Holland was Dickinson's steadiest correspondent.

Dickinson also met people through her brother and sister-in-law. Soon after their marriage, Austin and Susan Dickinson began to entertain frequently. Susan was socially ambitious and very accomplished. Austin had wide-ranging interests and many cultivated friends. In 1857, they hosted Ralph Waldo Emerson during his lecture series in Amherst. For Susan, this was a great honor. She later wrote, "I felt strangely elated to take his transcendental arm." They also entertained other prominent 19th-century men and women, including the novelist Harriet

Among the many accomplished people who visited Austin and Susan Dickinson at the Evergreens was Harriet Beecher Stowe, author of Uncle Tom's Cabin, *an immensely popular antislavery novel that was published in 1852.*

Beecher Stowe, author of *Uncle Tom's Cabin*; Stowe's brother, the nationally known preacher Henry Ward Beecher; and landscape architect Frederick Law Olmsted, who designed New York City's Central Park.

Samuel Bowles, editor of the Springfield Republican, *was a frequent guest at the Evergreens. During the 1850s, he published several of Dickinson's poems in the widely read newspaper.*

Emily Dickinson met Samuel Bowles and his wife during one of the intellectual gatherings at the Evergreens. Samuel Bowles was the influential editor of the *Springfield Republican*, which had a national readership. Dickinson saw Bowles frequently, and some biographers speculate she may even have been in love with him. Bowles was a handsome, charming man who was quite different from most of the men in Dickinson's circle. Aggressive, practical, and ambitious, he was a self-made man without a college education, and he was a secular man who stood outside the Congregational tradition of Dickinson's New England.

As editor of the *Springfield Republican*, Bowles published poetry and fiction in addition to news and editorials, and he was a potential patron if Dickinson had wanted to publish her work. He did in fact publish several of her poems, including one valentine, but his own taste ran to the sentimental poetry that was popular at the time, and Dickinson may have been unable to interest him in her more serious pieces.

Dickinson wrote poetry regularly during those years, and she began to organize her increasing store of finished work. She liked to bundle her poems into little packets that she created by carefully folding and sewing together several large sheets of paper. On each "page" she inscribed a clean copy of a poem. She had filled 40 of these booklets with poems by the time she died.

As Dickinson's approach to poetry became more serious, individual, and intense, her social circle grew smaller and smaller. She continued to venture as far as the Evergreens and took short trips to visit friends. But she had chosen a quiet life at home, and her daily routine was increasingly organized to suit the production of her poetry, which poured forth at a phenomenal rate in the next decade.

The original text of one Dickinson's best-known love poems, "Wild Nights—Wild Nights!"

S I X

"I Do Not Cross My Father's Ground"

By the beginning of the 1860s, Emily Dickinson had penned perhaps 200 poems; by the end of the decade, she had written more than 1,000. During those 10 years, she arranged her life in a pattern that she followed until her death. Withdrawing from society, she remained at the Homestead and devoted herself to her writing.

Years later, Emily's sister, Lavinia, remembered how the family lived together as "friendly and absolute monarchs." She described their respective domains: Emily "had to think—she was the only one of us who had that to do. . . . Father believed; and mother loved; and Austin had Amherst; and I had the family to keep track of." Lavinia's efforts ensured that Dickinson had the time "to think" and to write as she grew increasingly reclusive. The 1860s began with the sisters taking a trip to Connecticut to visit an old friend; in

1869, Dickinson stated firmly that "I do not cross my Father's ground to any House or Town."

During those years, Dickinson completed her break with the religion in which she was raised and stopped attending church. In 1860, she began a poem: "Some keep the Sabbath going to Church— / I keep it, staying at Home—." She continued to debate spiritual questions in her poetry and letters, but she stopped participating, even superficially, in the religious observances of her community. When questioned, she had an excuse for her unorthodox behavior: Her mother required constant care, and one of the two daughters had to be home at all times. In addition, Dickinson's own health was poor during those years.

Passionate emotions as well as ill health greatly troubled her. Dickinson wrote two more "Master" letters in

67

1861 and 1862. Each reveals her intense longing for the intended recipient. The second letter asserts that "I waited a long time—Master—but I can wait more—wait till my hazel hair is dappled—and you carry the cane—." A third letter, probably a first draft of a letter that may or may not have been sent, is especially desperate in its tone: "Master—open your life wide, and take me in forever, I will never be tired—I will never be noisy when you want to be still."

Dickinson expressed this longing for passion in a number of her poems. One of her most direct love poems was probably written in 1861:

> Wild Nights—Wild Nights!
> Were I with thee
> Wild Nights should be
> Our luxury!
> Futile—the Winds—
> To a Heart in port
> Done with the Compass—
> Done with the Chart!
> Rowing in Eden—
> Ah, the Sea!
> Might I but moor—Tonight
> In Thee!

The year this poem was composed is approximate because Dickinson never dated her work. Handwriting analysis provides the only clues as to when a particular poem was written. Fortunately for literary scholars, Dickinson's handwriting changed significantly over the years, and it is possible to assign specific years to her poems, although it is impossible to know whether she actually composed the poem in that year or merely recopied it. It seems that Dickinson took good care of her poems: She frequently recopied them neatly into her booklets and destroyed the earlier drafts.

Dickinson's work had grown extremely complex by the 1860s. Although she was still in her early thirties, she had been writing poetry for at least 10 years; her work had become sophisticated and well practiced. Some of her most powerful poems stem from this period, when her poetic abilities may have been at their height.

"I sing, as the Boy does by the Burying Ground," Dickinson explained in a letter, "—because I am afraid." Accordingly, mortality emerged as a chief topic in many of her poems, including the following verse, in which she imagines a dying person's last sensations:

> I heard a Fly buzz—when I died—
> The Stillness in the Room
> Was like the Stillness in the Air—
> Between the Heaves of Storm—
>
> The Eyes around—had wrung them dry—
> And Breaths were gathering firm
> For that last Onset—when the King
> Be witnessed—in the Room—
>
> I willed my Keepsakes—Signed away
> What portion of me be
> Assignable—and then it was
> There interposed a Fly—
>
> With Blue—uncertain stumbling Buzz—
> Between the light—and me—
> And then the Windows failed—and then
> I could not see to see—

Over the years, Dickinson sent 267 poems to her sister-in-law for editorial advice. Susan Dickinson was often too busy, however, to suggest how to improve the poet's verse.

Dickinson's nephew Edward Dickinson, who was born to Austin and Susan Dickinson in 1861.

For Dickinson, who did not believe in an afterlife in heaven, there was nothing at all romantic about one's physical decline into death. Indeed, the last line of the preceding poem hints at a particular worry: Dickinson's eyesight began to fail in the 1860s. She suffered from an eye disorder that made her extremely sensitive to light and caused periods of blurred vision or near blindness. Some of these symptoms had afflicted her in her twenties, but they worsened dramatically from 1861 to 1865. Doctors continually recommended that she rest her eyes, and one even prohibited her from reading for as long as eight months. In 1864 and 1865, she was forced to make two long trips to consult ophthalmologists (eye specialists) in Boston. She feared she was going blind.

For an educated woman such as Dickinson to live without her books must have been a severe trial, but for a poet of her abilities to contemplate a future without reading or writing must have been sheer torture. It was a crisis in her career, and she took several decisive steps. First, she composed poems at an extraordinary pace and recopied those she had already written. There are 86 poems in the handwriting of 1861; in 1862, she wrote or recopied 366 poems. Clearly, she tried to work as hard as she could for as long as she could. In 1863 and 1864, she continued to produce more than 100 poems a year. After this intense flurry of creativity, the number of poems written in a single year dwindled, and she maintained a steady pace of writing for the rest of her life.

Dickinson's illness eventually subsided, and she regained her eyesight. Yet when her vision was first troubling her, she began to seek out readers for her work. She sent "I taste a liquor never brewed—" to the *Springfield Republican*, and in May 1861 the newspaper published it under the title "The May-Wine." Although an editor added the title and changed the punctuation in the poem (against Dickinson's will—as was the case with her six other poems that appeared in print during her lifetime), Dickinson continued to pursue publication in the 1860s.

One of Dickinson's first steps was to turn to her sister-in-law, Susan Gilbert Dickinson, as a potential critic. In the fall of 1861, Dickinson sent three versions of the poem "Safe in their Alabaster Chambers" across the garden to Susan. Dickinson was trying to decide

on a final version of the poem, which was going to be published in the *Springfield Republican*.

This consultation between Dickinson and Susan Gilbert Dickinson is the only recorded instance of Dickinson's requesting literary help from anyone in her close circle. It also demonstrates Dickinson's high estimation of her sister-in-law's literary judgment. The first version of the poem that Dickinson sent to Susan read as follows:

> Safe in their Alabaster Chambers,
> Untouched by Morning
> And untouched by Noon—
> Sleep the meek members of the
>   Resurrection,
> Rafter of satin,
> And Roof of stone.
> Light laughs the breeze
> In her Castle above them—
> Babbles the Bee in a stolid Ear,
> Pipe the Sweet Birds in ignorant
>   cadence—
> Ah, what sagacity perished here!

After Susan criticized the second stanza of this poem, Dickinson sent over another version:

> Safe in their Alabaster Chambers—
> Untouched by Morning—
> And untouched by Noon—
> Lie the meek members of the
>   Resurrection—
> Rafter of Satin, and Roof of Stone!
> Grand go the years—in the
> Crescent—above them—Worlds
>   scoop their Arcs—
> And firmaments—row—
> Diadems—drop—and Doges—
>   surrender—
> Soundless as dots—on a Disc of
>   Snow—

Safe in their Alabaster
Chambers –
Untouched by Morning –
And untouched by Noon –
Lie the meek members of
the Resurrection –
Rafter of satin – and Roof
of stone –

Grand go the Years – in the
Crescent – above them –
Worlds scoop their Arcs –
And Firmaments – row –
Diadems – drop – and Doges –
surrender –
Soundless as dots – on a
Disc of snow –

Springs – shake the sills –
But – the Echoes – stiffen –
Hoar – is the window –

One of three different versions of "Safe in their Alabaster Chambers" that Dickinson sent to her sister-in-law, Susan Dickinson, for criticism in the fall of 1861. The initial version of the poem was published the following year in the Springfield Republican.

Again, Susan responded that "I am not suited dear Emily with the second verse—It is remarkable as the chain lightening that blinds us hot nights in the Southern sky but it does not go with the ghostly shimmer of the first verse as well as the other one—." Consequently, Dickinson sent over yet another version of the second stanza. The first version of the poem (the one Susan preferred) was published in the *Springfield Republican* in March 1862.

Over the years, Susan received 267 poems from Dickinson, but she was often too busy to give them the attention Dickinson demanded. On June 19, 1861, Austin and Susan had their first child, a son they named Edward, after his grandfather. In time, Susan became increasingly occupied with juggling her family responsibilities and her active social life.

Dickinson then turned to Thomas Wentworth Higginson as a potential adviser. On April 15, 1862, after reading his essay, "Letter to a Young Contributor," she sent him four poems, thus beginning her lifelong game of hide-and-seek with him. She often evaded his questions, seeming to follow her own advice in one of her poems: "Tell all the Truth but tell it slant—." She presented herself to Higginson as an inexperienced poet, when in fact she had already written hundreds of poems. She talked over his head, using cryptic language so that he could hardly understand her. She asked him to be her "Preceptor," then refused to follow his advice. Dickinson's attitude eventually

prompted Higginson's wife to complain, "Oh why do the insane so cling to you?"

Despite Dickinson's lack of cooperation, Higginson did his best to understand and encourage her work. As their correspondence progressed over the years, he remained confused about the role he could play in her development: "I have the greatest desire to see you, always feeling that perhaps if I could once take you by the hand I might be something to you; but till then you only enshroud yourself in this fiery mist & I cannot reach you, but only rejoice in the rare sparkles of light."

Higginson invited Dickinson to visit him in Boston early in their correspondence. He apparently wanted to introduce her into the literary circles in his hometown. But Dickinson was as eager to avoid the bustling literary scene as Higginson was anxious to have her enter it. She consistently turned down his invitations and suggested that he come to Amherst instead.

Eight years passed before Higginson finally took up her offer. In early August 1870, he realized that his travel plans were such that he would be passing near Amherst. At once, he wrote to Dickinson and asked if he could call on her. Dickinson assured him she would "be at Home and glad."

And so, in mid-August, Higginson made his way to the house where Emily Dickinson lived. Higginson later described it as "a large country lawyer's house, brown brick, with great trees & a garden." He was ushered into a "parlor dark & cool & stiffish" and waited for Dickinson's arrival. He soon heard "a step like a pattering child's in entry & in glided a little plain woman with two smooth bands of reddish hair." She was wearing, he recalled, "a very plain & exquisitely clean white pique [a dress of ribbed fabric] & a blue net worsted shawl. She came to me with two day lilies which she put in a sort of childlike way into my hand & said 'These are my introduction' in a soft frightened breathless childlike voice." Then she added, "Forgive me if I am frightened; I never see strangers & hardly know what I say."

Dickinson was not as shy as she suggested, however. "She talked soon & thenceforward continuously," Higginson recalled, adding that she spoke "for her own relief, and wholly without watching its effect on her hearer." She talked to Higginson mostly about books, concentrating on the subject that brought them together: poetry. "If I read a book [and] it makes my whole body so cold no fire ever can warm me I know *that* is poetry," she told him. "If I feel physically as if the top of my head were taken off, I know *that* is poetry. These are the only way I know it." Higginson later said of Dickinson, "I never was with any one who drained my nerve power so much."

Higginson had hoped that meeting Dickinson would help him understand her difficult poems. Instead, her behavior only added to his confusion. She acted like a child, yet her speech was so complex he could hardly follow her.

She claimed to be meek and humble, yet her poems were fierce, passionate, and powerful. Twenty years later, Higginson concluded that still "she was much too enigmatical a being for me to solve in an hour's interview."

Dickinson was as enigmatic in letter as she was in person. Higginson saved the letters she wrote to him, and they furnish many examples of the style he found so baffling. They also hint at his responses to her poetry (a particularly valuable source of information because most of his letters to her were not preserved). One aspect of her poetry he found particularly odd was her experimentation with meter (the rhythmical pattern of syllables stressed in lines of verse); her meters were of a sort not often found in 19th-century popular poetry. Many of her poems are composed of alternating lines of eight syllables and six syllables. Called "common meter," this is the meter of American nursery rhymes and Congregational hymns.

Dickinson also played with traditional rhyme schemes. She frequently replaced them with partial rhymes or words that sounded alike but did not quite rhyme. Sometimes, she used eye rhymes: words that are spelled as if they rhyme, such as *word* and *lord*. On occasion, she did not make use of rhymes at all.

No matter what meter and rhyme scheme she worked in, Dickinson paid meticulous attention to the words she chose. She tested and discarded a great number until she found the one she

Thomas Wentworth Higginson with his daughter. He said of Dickinson, "We corresponded at varying intervals, she always persistently keeping up this attitude of 'Scholar,' and assuming on my part of preceptorship which it is almost needless to say did not exist. Always glad to hear her 'recite,' as she called it, I soon abandoned all attempt to guide in the slightest degree this extraordinary nature, and simply accepted her confidences, giving as much as I could of what might interest her in return."

Emily Fowler Ford, a childhood friend of Dickinson's and a poet as well. It is possible that Ford helped Dickinson publish a few of her poems in New York City newspapers during the 1860s.

considered best for that poem. She once wrote, "A Word dropped careless on a Page . . . Infection in the sentence breeds."

Dickinson's tone and aim were as unusual as the extraordinary care she took in selecting her words. Most of the woman poets who published their work in the popular magazines of the day usually wrote descriptive poems about sentimental topics, such as flowers, heaven, romance, and tragic death. Dickinson treated these matters, too, but her aim was less descriptive than analytical, and her tone was very often fierce. The feelings she described and incorporated into her work were intensely personal, which may have disturbed most readers. In addition, Dickinson's broad education and extensive knowledge of the Bible made her references difficult for many people to grasp.

One of her childhood friends, Emily Fowler, became a published poet who evidently found Dickinson's poetry difficult to comprehend. Although the two rarely wrote to each other after Fowler married and moved to New York City, Emily Fowler Ford and her husband may have been instrumental in helping Dickinson publish some poems in New York City newspapers during the 1860s. Nonetheless, after Dickinson's death, Ford wrote a memorial poem, "Eheu! Emily Dickinson!," in which she bemoaned her friend's life of "shadow." Ford always insisted that Dickinson chose seclusion only because her poetry was never publicly successful.

Several other poems of Dickinson's were published in the 1860s. The *Springfield Republican* printed "Blazing in gold and quenching in purple" in 1864 and "A Narrow Fellow in the Grass," which was submitted to the newspaper by Susan Gilbert Dickinson without the poet's knowledge, in 1866. All together, five of the seven poems published while Dickinson was alive appeared in the 1860s in the *Springfield Republican*. Although Dickinson may have initially approached Higginson to investigate the possibility of publishing her poetry, she abandoned the idea a few years later. She never again actively sought publication of her work.

A SELECTION OF POEMS BY
EMILY DICKINSON

Much madness is divinest sense
To a discerning eye;
Much sense the starkest madness.
'T is the majority
In this, as all, prevails.
Assent, and you are sane;
Demur,—you're straightway dangerous,
And handled with a chain.

I like to see it lap the miles,
And lick the valleys up,
And stop to feed itself at tanks;
And then, prodigious, step

Around a pile of mountains,
And, supercilious, peer
In shanties by the sides of roads;
And then a quarry pare

To fit its sides, and crawl between,
Complaining all the while
In horrid, hooting stanza;
Then chase itself down hill

And neigh like Boanerges;
Then, punctual as a star,
Stop—docile and omnipotent—
At its own stable door.

I taste a liquor never brewed,
From tankards scooped in pearl;
Not all the vats upon the Rhine
Yield such an alcohol!

Inebriate of air am I,
And debauchee of dew,
Reeling, through endless summer days,
From inns of molten blue.

When landlords turn the drunken bee
Out of the foxglove's door,
When butterflies renounce their drams,
I shall but drink the more!

Till seraphs swing their snowy hats,
And saints to windows run,
To see the little tippler
Leaning against the sun!

Hope is the thing with feathers
That perches in the soul,
And sings the tune without the words,
And never stops at all,

And sweetest in the gale is heard;
And sore must be the storm
That could abash the little bird
That kept so many warm.

I've heard it in the chillest land,
And on the strangest sea;
Yet, never, in extremity,
It asked a crumb of me.

I dwell in Possibility
A fairer house than Prose,
More numerous of windows,
Superior of doors.

Of chambers, as the cedars—
Impregnable of eye;
And for an everlasting roof
The gables of the sky.

Of visitors—the fairest—
For occupation—this—
The spreading wide my narrow hands
To gather Paradise.

Because I could not stop for Death,
He kindly stopped for me;
The carriage held but just ourselves
And Immortality.

We slowly drove, he knew no haste,
And I had put away
My labor, and my leisure too,
For his civility.

We passed the school where children played
At wrestling in a ring;
We passed the fields of gazing grain,
We passed the setting sun.

We paused before a house that seemed
A swelling of the ground;
The roof was scarcely visible,
The cornice but a mound.

Since then 't is centuries; but each
Feels shorter than the day
I first surmised the horses' heads
Were toward eternity.

Tell all the Truth but tell it slant—
Success in Circuit lies
Too bright for our infirm Delight
The Truth's superb surprise
As Lightning to the Children eased
With explanation kind
The Truth must dazzle gradually
Or every man be blind—

Dickinson was deeply grieved by the death of her father, Edward, in 1874. His passing marked the beginning of a number of personal blows to the poet.

SEVEN

"Blow Has Followed Blow"

In 1872, after serving as the treasurer of Amherst College for 40 years, Edward Dickinson resigned from the post because of ill health. His condition improved enough the following year to allow him to return to Boston as a member of the Massachusetts General Court. But in 1874 his health took a turn for the worse. In a grief-stricken letter to her Norcross cousins, Emily Dickinson described her last moments with her father:

> The last Afternoon that my Father lived, though with no premonition—I preferred to be with him, and invented an absence for Mother, Vinnie being asleep. He seemed peculiarly pleased as I oftenest stayed with myself, and remarked as the Afternoon withdrew, he "would like it not to end." His pleasure almost embarrassed me and my Brother coming—I suggested they walk. Next morning I woke him for the train—and saw him no more.

Emily was traumatized by her father's death, and in her sorrow she secluded herself even more. She did not even attend his funeral. Distraught, she complained to her cousins that "though it is many nights, my mind never comes home."

Two years after her father's death, Dickinson wrote again to her cousins: "I dream about father every night, always a different dream, and forget what I am doing daytimes, wondering where he is." Although her relationship with her father may have been undemonstrative, she sorely felt his absence. Lavinia Dickinson later commented that she and Emily had feared their father while he was alive but learned to love him after his death.

One year after their father's death, their mother suffered a stroke that left her bedridden for the next seven years. Not surprisingly, these family crises

A view of Dickinson's bedroom at the Homestead. She often put cookies in the basket on the window sill and lowered it to children outside.

took their toll on Dickinson's poetry. She still wrote exquisite poems, but not, as years earlier, in a flood of words. More and more, she spent her time writing letters, and they became her chief means of communicating with the outside world.

As her own world continued to narrow, Dickinson had little interest in getting her poems published. When Thomas Wentworth Higginson recommended her work to the editor of a women's magazine, Dickinson frostily rejected the idea. The last poem to be published during her lifetime appeared in print in 1878, thanks to the help of one of her Amherst Academy classmates.

Helen Fiske had known Dickinson when they were both children in Amherst, although they were never close friends. Fiske left Amherst for boarding school, and when Dickinson next heard of her, Fiske had married E. B. Hunt.

Widowed during the Civil War, Helen Fiske Hunt pursued a writing career that culminated in the publication of a highly acclaimed volume of poetry in 1870.

Through Higginson, Hunt resumed her acquaintanceship with Dickinson, and the two exchanged letters and poems throughout the 1870s. In 1875, when her literary reputation was cresting, Hunt married W. S. Jackson, and Helen Hunt Jackson became a household name. Perhaps the most popular female poet in the United States at that time, she was then also one of the few people to perceive Dickinson's genius.

Jackson loved Emily Dickinson's poetry, and she continually urged Dickinson to share it with the world. In 1876, Jackson scolded her: "You are a great poet—and it is a wrong to the day you live in, that you will not sing aloud." She added, "When you are what men call dead, you will be sorry you were so stingy." Jackson had a specific project in mind. She wrote to Dickinson several times to persuade her that she should contribute some of her work to a poetry anthology that was going to be published in Boston. Jackson especially wanted Dickinson to submit the following poem:

> Success is counted sweetest
> By those who ne'er succeed.
> To comprehend a nectar
> Requires sorest need.
> Not one of all the purple Host
> Who took the Flag today
> Can tell the definition
> So clear of Victory
> As he defeated—dying—
> On whose forbidden ear
> The distant strains of triumph
> Burst agonized and clear!

Dickinson hesitated in giving her permission to publish the poem. She asked Higginson's opinion of the idea, all the while insisting that her work was not good enough to be published. But Jackson did not give up. During a two-year period, she pressed her case in several letters and two visits to Amherst.

Helen Hunt Jackson, a nationally known poet who also hailed from Amherst, was a great admirer and supporter of Dickinson's work.

It remains unclear whether Dickinson eventually gave her permission to have the poem published or whether Jackson simply inferred Dickinson's consent from her silence. In any event, the poem appeared under the title "Success" in the 1878 anthology *A Masque of Poets*. The literary world immediately attributed the anonymously written poem to Ralph Waldo Emerson.

Like Higginson, Jackson was one of the few people who saw Dickinson during her later years. But unlike Higginson, Jackson was always direct with Dickinson. When Jackson did not understand a poem, she sent it back to Dickinson. And when she thought Dickinson strange, she said so. Of one visit, Jackson wrote: "I feel as if I had been very impertinent that day in speaking to you as I did,—accusing you of living away from the sunlight—and telling you that you looked ill, . . . but really you looked so white and moth-like! Your hand felt like such a wisp in mine that you frightened me. I felt like a great ox talking to a white moth, and begging it to come and eat grass with me to see if it could not turn itself into beef! How stupid."

Jackson's faith in Dickinson's work never wavered, however, and in 1884 she offered to become Dickinson's literary executor. But Helen Hunt Jackson died the following year, before she could arrange to have the poems published.

During those years of deaths and illnesses, there was at least one source of joy in Dickinson's life: her romance

Judge Otis Phillips Lord, a family friend who was almost 20 years older than Dickinson, received the first of many love letters from the poet in the mid-1870s. Thereafter, they carried on a weekly correspondence.

with Judge Otis Phillips Lord. She once described Judge Lord as her father's closest friend; he and Edward Dickinson were both lawyers who had served successfully in state politics and were conservative members of the Whig party. Judge Lord was an Amherst College graduate who often returned to the Massachusetts town for school reunions. During the early 1870s, he and his wife were frequent visitors to the Homestead. After Edward Dickinson's death in 1874, they continued to visit the Homestead, keeping up their friendship with Edward's children.

An envelope addressed to Judge Otis Phillips Lord by Dickinson.

During one of those visits, Judge Lord's relationship with Emily Dickinson blossomed into something deeper than friendship. In 1878, one year after Lord's wife died, Dickinson wrote the earliest of her surviving love letters to him. She exclaimed in one letter, "I confess that I love him—I rejoice that I love him—I thank the maker of Heaven and Earth—that gave him me to love—." Dickinson was 46 years old and Lord was 65 at the time.

Because Judge Lord lived in eastern Massachusetts and Dickinson never traveled, they communicated every week with each other through letters. Whether Lord proposed marriage to her, and whether Dickinson accepted his proposal, is not revealed in their correspondence. She had spent years establishing a daily routine that allowed her to write poetry, and her mother still needed nursing. Moreover, Lord's relatives were extremely opposed to his remarrying. As a result, Lord's relationship with Dickinson, which lasted until his death in 1884, never led to a betrothal.

Death had also intruded upon Dickinson's life a couple of years earlier: In

Dickinson's nephew Gilbert Dickinson, who died in 1883. The poet had been especially fond of him.

1882, her mother finally succumbed to her illness. Emily did not feel any relief that her mother's ordeal had finally ended. Instead, the poet was as upset by her mother's death as she had been by her father's passing eight years before. "Her dying," she wrote, "feels to me like many kinds of Cold—at times electric, at times benumbing—then a trackless waste."

Mabel Loomis Todd, who was living in Amherst at the time, later remarked of Emily and Lavinia Dickinson that "their mother, quiet, gentle, little lady, died during the middle of November 1882, without causing a perceptible ripple on the surface of anyone's life, or giving concern to any of her family." But Todd was wrong. Despite her occasional bitter comments about her mother in earlier years, Emily later said: "We were never intimate Mother and Children while she was our Mother, but Mines in the same Ground meet by tunneling, and when she became our Child, the Affection came." As with her father, Dickinson's feelings for her mother were not fully expressed until after her death.

"Blow has followed blow, till the wondering terror of the Mind clutches what is left," Dickinson wrote after her mother's death. Indeed, between 1874 and 1882, both of her parents died, as well as her old friends Samuel Bowles, Josiah Holland, and Charles Wadsworth. Unfortunately, there were more blows to come. Dickinson suffered through the death of her young nephew Gilbert in 1883, Judge Lord in 1884, and Helen Hunt Jackson in 1885. Her sister, Lavinia, was quite ill in 1883, and her brother, Austin, was seriously sick with malaria several times during the decade.

To make matters worse, there was often tension between the two Dickinson homes. Emily Dickinson frequently found herself caught between her sister's anger at Susan Gilbert Dickinson and her own abiding respect for her girlhood friend. Lavinia seemed to blame her sister-in-law for her tempestuous relationship with both Austin and Emily. The various parties never spoke about their feelings of resentment. Yet these family frictions would continue after the poet's death, and they would ultimately affect the development of her literary reputation.

Dickinson often wore this white dress during her years as a recluse.

EIGHT

The Myth of Amherst

In the fall of 1881, Mabel Loomis Todd wrote an enthusiastic letter to her parents about her new home in Amherst. Included in this description were her first impressions of Emily Dickinson: "I must tell you about the *character* of Amherst. It is a lady whom the people call the *Myth*. She is a sister of Mr. Dickinson's & seems to be the climax of all the family oddity. She has not been outside of her own house in fifteen years, except once to see a new church, when she crept out at night, & viewed it by moonlight."

Throughout the 1880s, stories about the poet continued to multiply. Neighbors repeated these tales to each other, and visitors to Amherst hoped that they would be fortunate enough to glimpse Dickinson's ghostly presence at the Homestead. Her eccentricities

were well known by then: She never left her family's home, she refused to see strangers; she entertained friends from behind half-closed doors or from the dark recesses of a stairwell; and she always wore white. Although Dickinson loved children, she seldom let them see her, preferring to lower candy and treats to them from her window. The most intriguing rumor about Dickinson was that she had had a tragic love affair in her youth that caused her to renounce the world in despair.

Mabel Loomis Todd was fascinated by such stories, especially when she heard about Dickinson's literary talent. An accomplished young woman married to an Amherst College professor, Todd soon began socializing with the leading intellectuals of the town, including Emily Dickinson's brother,

A close friend of the Dickinson family, Mabel Loomis Todd became the first person to edit Emily Dickinson's cache of poems.

Mabel Loomis Todd (standing, center) with her husband, David Peck Todd (far right), and Susan Dickinson (seated, center). They were members of a social group known as the Shutesbury School of Philosophy.

Austin, and his wife, Susan Gilbert Dickinson. It was at the Evergreens that Todd first heard Dickinson's poems, which she declared were "full of power."

After hearing about Todd's comment, Dickinson began sending poems and flowers to her during the next few months. Then, in September 1882, Todd was honored with an invitation to visit the Homestead. Dickinson, always fond of music, had heard about Todd's fine singing voice and wanted

her to give a recital. On the designated date, Todd went to the house and gave a performance, but she did not see Dickinson. "It was odd to think, as my voice rang out through the big silent house that Miss Emily in her weird white dress was outside in the shadow hearing every word," Todd wrote about the incident, then added—incorrectly, as it turned out—"I know I shall yet see her."

As Mabel Loomis Todd became increasingly friendly with the Dickinsons, she found herself pulled into what has been called the "War Between the Houses." All was not well in both the Evergreens and the Homestead. Austin and Susan's marriage was failing, and Lavinia was feuding constantly with her sister-in-law.

When Todd first arrived in Amherst with her husband, David Peck Todd, Lavinia and Susan Gilbert Dickinson competed for her friendship. Mabel Loomis Todd grew close to Susan Gilbert Dickinson for a year, but by the autumn of 1882 their friendship had

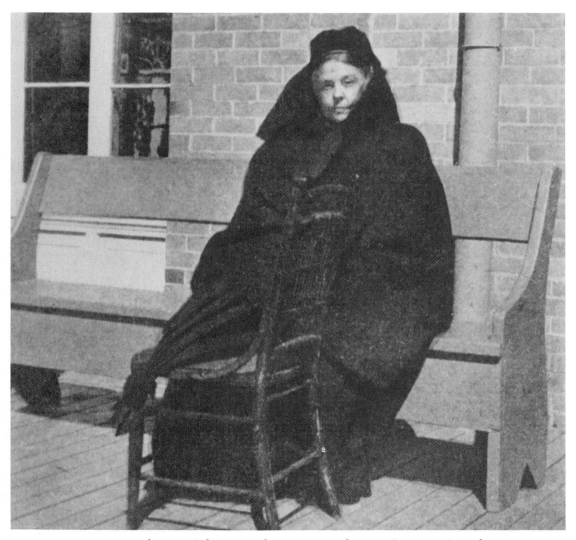

Susan Dickinson (above) and Lavinia Dickinson (opposite) in the mid-1890s. Their strained relationship ultimately led to a lengthy delay in the publication of Emily Dickinson's collected poems.

become strained, and Todd began to spend more of her time with Lavinia and Austin Dickinson. Then, on the day after her first visit to the Homestead, Todd and Austin Dickinson embarked on a love affair that lasted until his death in 1895. The troubled air around the Evergreens and the Homestead grew heavier.

Neither Mabel nor Austin bothered to hide their relationship from their spouses, and soon the whole town knew about the romance. Nevertheless, no one in the family talked about it, and there is no mention of it in Emily Dickinson's surviving letters. Years later, Todd's daughter repeated her mother's belief that "Emily always respected real emotion."

Amid these family tensions, Dickinson became steadily weaker. In the spring of 1884, she had her first attack of the kidney disease that would ultimately kill her. A year and a half later, her illness caused her to be confined to bed.

On May 13, 1886, Emily Dickinson lost consciousness. She died on May 15, at the age of 55. Shortly before her death, she wrote to her Norcross cousins: "Little Cousins,—Called back.—Emily."

Dickinson's funeral service was held on May 19 and was capped by Thomas Wentworth Higginson reading from Emily Brontë's last poem. Dickinson's body was buried in the west cemetery, next to her parents' graves. Susan Gilbert Dickinson wrote the obituary that appeared in the *Springfield Republican*: "Very few in the village,

except among the older inhabitants, knew Miss Emily personally, although the facts of her seclusion and her intellectual brilliancy were familiar Amherst traditions. . . . As she passed on in life, her sensitive nature shrank from much personal contact with the world,

William Dean Howells, America's leading man of letters at the end of the 19th century. He helped launch Dickinson's literary reputation by praising the first edition of her poems as a "distinctive addition" to American art.

and more and more turned to her own large wealth of individual resources for companionship."

Shortly afterward, Lavinia Dickinson made her momentous discovery of her sister's poems. Upon the publication of the first edition of Emily Dickinson's *Poems* in 1890, William Dean Howells, perhaps the nation's most influential man of letters at that time, commended the volume as a "distinctive addition"

to American literature. Praise was not universal, however. One American poet who reviewed the first volume of Dickinson's poetry complained in an 1892 issue of the *Atlantic Monthly* that "for the most part the ideas totter and toddle, not having learned to walk. In spite of this, several of the quatrains are curiously touching, they have such a pathetic air of yearning to be poems."

For the most part, though, Dickinson's reputation as a poet continued to rise, and the imagination of the American public was seized by the Myth of Amherst. Mabel Loomis Todd was besieged with requests for information about the poet and went on several lecture tours to discuss Dickinson's life and work. Austin and Lavinia Dickinson spent the last years of their life denying that the bizarre stories about their sister were true. Lavinia even wrote a forceful letter to the *Boston Transcript* in 1894, in response to a fanciful account of her sister's life: "Emily's so called 'withdrawal from general society,' for which she never cared, was only a happen. . . . Emily chose this part and, finding the life with her books and nature so congenial, continued to live it."

But the popular image of the mystery woman only broadened Dickinson's appeal for American readers. They clamored for more information about her. Todd and Higginson brought out a second series of poems in 1891, and Todd compiled, edited, and published two volumes of Dickinson's collected letters in 1894. Two years later, Todd brought out yet another volume of po-

Austin Dickinson, unhappy in his marriage to his wife, Susan, maintained a romance with Mabel Loomis Todd that lasted for 13 years.

Martha Dickinson Bianchi, the poet's niece (left), and Millicent Todd Bingham, Mabel Loomis Todd's daughter (right), who played pivotal roles in arranging for the publication of all of Emily Dickinson's verse.

ems by Dickinson. All three volumes of poetry sold well.

Just as the third volume of poems appeared in print, the tensions that had been brewing between Todd and the Dickinsons over the past decade came suddenly to a head, bringing the task of collecting, sorting, and publishing Dickinson's poems and correspondence to a halt. After Austin's death in 1895, Lavinia Dickinson, who had been closely working with Todd on sorting out the poems, disputed Todd's right to a piece of land that Austin had given her. Lavinia brought a lawsuit against Todd and also changed her mind about letting Todd edit the poems.

After being forced to return the land, Todd vowed to have nothing more to do with the Dickinson family. She packed up the poems she had been editing and left them in her attic. They remained there for more than 30 years. "What a novel could be written about the Dickinson family," said a neighbor who had witnessed the worst of the backbiting.

It was not until well into the 20th century, through the separate efforts of Dickinson's niece, Martha Dickinson Bianchi, and Todd's daughter, Millicent Todd Bingham, that work was resumed on the poems. New collections were published in 1935, 1937, and 1945. Then, in 1955, almost 70 years after Dickinson's death, *The Poems of Emily Dickinson*—all 1,775 of her poems, in their original, unedited form—was finally published.

As Dickinson's stature as a poet has grown over the years, her readers have demanded more and more information about her. Yet it is still her poems that offer the most tantalizing glimpse into her rich and intensely private inner life. Indeed, she said pointedly of her verse:

This is my letter to the World
That never wrote to Me—
The simple News that Nature told—
With tender Majesty
Her Message is committed
To Hands I cannot see—
For love of Her—Sweet—countrymen—
Judge tenderly—of Me.

FURTHER READING

Bloom, Harold, ed. *Emily Dickinson.* New York: Chelsea House, 1985.

Franklin, Ralph W., ed. *The Manuscript Books of Emily Dickinson.* Cambridge: Harvard University Press, 1981.

Gilbert, Sandra M., and Susan Gubar. *The Madwoman in the Attic: The Woman Writer and the Nineteenth-century Literary Imagination.* New Haven: Yale University Press, 1979.

Johnson, Thomas H., ed. *The Complete Poems of Emily Dickinson.* Boston: Little, Brown, 1960.

———. *The Letters of Emily Dickinson, 3 vols.* Cambridge: Harvard University Press, 1958.

Luce, William. *The Belle of Amherst: A Play Based on the Life of Emily Dickinson.* Boston: Houghton Mifflin, 1976.

Rich, Adrienne. *On Lies, Secrets, and Silence: Selected Prose 1966–1978.* New York: Norton, 1979.

Sewall, Richard B. *The Life of Emily Dickinson, 2 vols.* New York: Farrar, Straus & Giroux, 1974.

Thayer, Bonita. *Emily Dickinson.* New York: Watts, 1989.

Woolf, Cynthia Griffin. *Emily Dickinson.* Reading, MA: Addison-Wesley, 1988.

CHRONOLOGY

Dec. 10, 1830	Emily Elizabeth Dickinson born in Amherst, Massachusetts, at the Homestead
1840	Dickinsons move from the Homestead to house on North Pleasant Street, in Amherst; Dickinson enrolls in Amherst Academy
1847	Enrolls in Mount Holyoke Female Seminary
1850	Amherst College student newspaper publishes a Dickinson valentine verse
1852	*Springfield Republican* publishes a second Dickinson valentine verse
1855	Dickinson visits her father in Washington, D.C.; Dickinsons move back into the Homestead
1861	*Springfield Republican* publishes "I taste a liquor never brewed"
1862	*Springfield Republican* publishes "Safe in their Alabaster Chambers" and "Blazing in gold and quenching in purple"; Dickinson sends first letter and four poems to Thomas Wentworth Higginson; *New York Magazine* publishes Dickinson's "Some keep the Sabbath going to church"
1865	*Springfield Republican* publishes "A narrow fellow in the grass"
1870	Higginson visits Dickinson in Amherst
1874	Dickinson's father dies in Boston
1875	Dickinson's mother suffers a stroke
1876	Helen Hunt Jackson invites Dickinson to submit a poem to an anthology of poetry
1878	Dickinson's romance with Judge Otis Phillips Lord begins; "Success is counted sweetest" appears in *A Masque of Poets*
1882	Mabel Loomis Todd visits the Homestead; Dickinson's mother dies
May 15, 1886	Emily Dickinson dies in Amherst
1890	First volume of Dickinson's *Poems* published, edited by Mabel Loomis Todd and Thomas Wentworth Higginson, printed in Boston

INDEX

INDEX

Victoria Olsen, a graduate of Barnard College and a lifetime resident of New York City, is currently studying English literature at Stanford University. She is also the author of *The Dutch Americans* in Chelsea House's PEOPLES OF NORTH AMERICA series.

❖   ❖   ❖

Matina S. Horner is president of Radcliffe College and associate professor of psychology and social relations at Harvard University. She is best known for her studies of women's motivation, achievement, and personality development. Dr. Horner serves on several national boards and advisory councils, including those of the National Science Foundation, Time Inc., and the Women's Research and Education Institute. She earned her B. A. from Bryn Mawr College and Ph.D. from the University of Michigan, and holds honorary degrees from many colleges and universities, including Mount Holyoke, Smith, Tufts, and the University of Pennsylvania.